HOW TO LAUGH

HOW TO LAUGH

Miles Champion

ADVENTURES IN POETRY

Cover and drawings by Trevor Winkfield
Book design by typeslowly

Some of these poems first appeared in *Aufgabe, Bombay Gin, The Brooklyn Rail, The Capilano Review, the claudius app, Critical Quarterly, dcpoetry* (In Your Ear), *DREAMBOAT, I Saw Johnny Yesterday, No: A Journal of the Arts, not enough night, onedit, PN Review, Primary Writing, Shiny, wildhoneypress* and *Zoland Poetry*; in the chapbook *Eventually* (Tuscaloosa, AL: The Rest, 2008); the anthologies *onsets* (Willowdale, ON: The Gig, 2004) and *The i.e. Reader* (Baltimore, MD: Narrow House, 2009); and the exhibition catalogue *Figuring Color* (Ostfildern, Germany / Boston, MA: Hatje Cantz / The Institute of Contemporary Art, 2012). "Air Ball" and the accompanying drawing were published as *Tolling Elves* 15 (London: 2004); "Providence" was published as an artist's edition / portfolio (in collaboration with Jane South) by Sienese Shredder Editions (New York: 2008); "Wet Flatware" and the accompanying drawing were published as part of *Monday 2nd April 2007 Mag* (New York: 2007); "Wheels" was published as *Poetics Plus Broadside #3* by the Poetics Program of the University at Buffalo, The State University of New York (2007).

Adventures in Poetry titles are distributed to the trade through Zephyr Press by Consortium Book Sales and Distribution [cbsd.com] & Small Press Distribution [spdbooks.org]

ISBN 978-0-9761612-7-1
ADVENTURESINPOETRY.COM

for Rachel

CONTENTS

The handicap is perfection

—MICHAEL GIZZI

WHERE TO WRITE

So going around to get
in

The composition, exact
The grouping calmer yet
more precise

a profitable exercise
resting on nothing
wet cups leave blisters
no dice

there is a voice
nearby

suppose it is obtrusive
but we
play
nice

the use of prefabricated senses
restores grip

able to fondle the handle
likeness
brings warmth of attack
its own lips

while the tune is held by
a few assistants

the blotter questions the widening
shape

what balloon famously
lost its speech

white of the cloud
exudation of cumbersome
parts holding tears

the right place
should have cloisters

or at least a home depot

paint some of your chairs
expose others

before that show of colour
a more nervous furniture likes
to prepare

the tune lacks
polish

which closet vegetable says green is wrong

collars, steamed
and in
the dressing room
salad tongs

the potato sweeter
the social
eater
more pale than hurt
asking
why is there no occasion

the stiff, paper plate
moisture cakes
hat season

agreeably stultifying
peace
between two folds
suggests a crust
bolsters

secure a yellow corner
plaster
flake on cigarette end

makes an
opportune
blend

there having been jack
cheese on
everything else

seen cows shaving
with better lather
cream of single
take or leaf

where each double negative answers
both sides make four points
points that squares show
suggestions

that there might be a simple extension
wings
a nausea that medicines can
taste

if they like a magazine
the patients increase circulation
see chart attached

it makes easy reading
certainly
does this change?
I think so
a symbol adjustment to do with dates or figs
pleasure at any rate between curves and outlines
and a suitably cheap
gown that fits

to submit old claims
promptly
alter your birthday
don't forget to sign

as pedestrian clergymen cross
chickens extract meaning
perhaps pecking at a string bean
to be contiguous

later if it isn't dangerous
an asparagus
meets breakfast eggs
mixed up in counter action
with a pan

SKETCH FOR RELIEF

These lines

        Bare and

Drawn beyond

        Criticism

I check

        Faults with reverie

They loosen

        Us out of

Our heads

LOLITA IN WONDERLAND

I step leisurely toward surprises. I limit work to custom jobs inside a doll. I shake in my shoes when a cocktail develops. I've got to act tiny, with a network for dabbing at contracts to get rid of germs. My eyeball squeaks like a balloon.

Sleep, with its room key dangling from a yawn, arrives at my face with a writ for nonpayment of working features while persistent night opens to swallow a philter. I tweak loose the threshold. There's ample space for a negative image but it's quiet and uptight, like when a self-made reclining nude said fuck you to Picasso.

The best money catches nice immediate drugs. A bent cop draws back a leafy smell. I should see if my corkscrew has a biological use. Why was Mozart covered in thick fur? Does smoke have children? Which armpit toy is mostly glass? I smash through the picturesque, where the cows go sha-boom, to suck on a hatchet. Might go looking for the fish slice.

It's what happens when a gunman creates a lipstick, it feels great in your hand then you lose it. Kurosawa's a shrub, Hammett a rinsing glass. I film my teeth.

In Sweden once this guy jiggled shrimps in yoghurt, contracted leprosy and became a nun. His father had a silly name for welding struts to a can. Ice cubes in paraffin. The dishwasher crossbow. The bullet with increased leisure. I seem first to shoot and then exploit a photogenic smear.

I wake to a tiny church bell, bring it to my lips and say a blanket word. An orderly hoses a jigsaw. I bake a sponge. I take down a glossary of forms. I go mad before nature and am withdrawn at lunch. I teach death, using my own end to point to the mechanism while my keeper straddles the butt-piece. I plait thongs until they give a vague impression of belt. I sing the body leather.

Actual contact would make any scientist dirty up there, fidget with a bar of soap, turn a few cartwheels, borrow a vacuum cleaner, fetch some ether, make the dead speak, then get lost, return to invented childhood, become a dreamer, walk into Torquay, miss the gig, hear the grass grow, feel out of it, hide behind a lettuce, know all things, go back inside, climb the social ladder, dick an actor, cancel the milk, ring Charlie Korngold, mistake a lipless jug for a quasi-theatre, bleach a pair of jeans, help a jockey quit by using the last of the vaseline, ask if "wabe" is stone, hold a piece of it the wrong way less than six inches from a natural bowl with a stage. The plastic world won't keep, desserts turn into stiff waves. A monster decorates the labyrinth. Two deck chairs full of rock plants beguile a small deer. A bit of flex spills out of a bra. I paint it, pink.

Down in the ping-pong room I rotate my hands, as if screwing a moth into jogging pants. I get my tools to step out while my privacy guards the flashlight. A bead constrains the sweat on my face. The moth fits the brief. It sits back while I explain what prose is, activating the plot in the process. I incubate a musical phrase in my mouth, separating the white from the notes. The song expands priapically, a ball sometimes resting on it. A workman patches the leak-back from a mental checkmark, an ark on dribble.

The hermit crab, I concede, is a self-involved lookout at best. The ancients thought its meat was a guest. In medieval days they contemplated its bust. This might sound silly but I gape at sculptors, find their workshops attractive. I dream that my special hole can machine a vegetable. Washday. I give my sweater to a girl on the beach. The shape of a custard pie looms over Broadway, fabulous, grief-proof, unreal.

Film space could learn a lot from puff pastry. Air is sexy—the kind that inflates. Popcorn repeats itself. The critic picks and discards seeds while a stock type studies the camera box, prospecting for ingredients. I masticate from a disinterested vantage point. I come to a head in which events are shown, tilting the final scene so the credits roll.

UNDER HEAVY MANNERS

They were visibly altered.

IN THE AIR

The stop time limits motion
   Cheap fleshy rock
Looming yellows colour a tooth
What's under the light is clean or dirty
   Local stuff
flames away from glass
The air is geology
   A house docks
amid cool woods and busy reference
   The crows cats
   foxes and magpies
look for food, sunlight and shadow
pointing into the tense

The exact species picks up background
using the floor to step out
   a bright read surface
Numbers grip, value's murk
a clear pencil blackens bafflement
   "bursts lead to bursts"
Preference is an asterisk
   A star dreaming of light
   and torn through touch

A primer is noting the mismatch
Several beach chairs covered in snow
   of some aerial wrench

nailed by its stalk to the pole
    Night siphons mirror
a hot wind and party guests traced by pheromones
    Each hole is solid
bubbles into view against the window
As the sun comes on and we think to
    transduce coolness
By kissing force goodbye
    This conscience
a lucky official sense of depth

    Angular lassitude
with the "whirr" of a person
nailed to its closed tip a sentiment
    yielding states
human jets strip out of the bandshell
pink rubber dovetailed with night haze
    unbutton, press release
the ripe cycles got collected
    names in their celibacy
    questioning space

    The eye as target
    no rival teams
    "block the sight"
The written region calls spontaneous
Chains link means, ring mute bells
    Forming spheres
bake until golden
Doubt tunes division

in an "evaporating matrix"
   Deep sides resist
   a flat thumb
projecting a simulated hook

Invisible method "envelops photographs as
   much as literature"
A short bead perspires
   The flames are white
their shapes stuck before noting
   the designated exit
One flicks through a transitive corridor
   Sense data fills
   from its amber lining
in range of discoloured routine

Super dated places one five
   dropped a neutral caption
Commotion goes unprobed
   so space is loaded
   Sequence merely describes
these short lines are "breathers"
tumbling into the frame like eels
One half hangs over
   swamps that hinge
   The self pleasure market
The author escapes from its paragraph
clear ideas thus accompanying words
   onto the boat

COLOUR IN HUYSMANS

Time is an instrument of construction

          no use to

Already putting the chair in a room or ocean

              abstrusely stitched

Invention is obstinacy

            sitting on memory's blade

Notched by unfolding an inner transparency

               in Haikuesque tweed

Pocket giants blot out the sunlight

            unpluck each

To pronounce the roofless distort the bird drum

                absent then featherlike

The dunce stool over the stairway

             Thick as paint

Bandaging the sieve with greater capacity

                acid's vacuum

Setting the shape of facts to the myth of their vapour

             the scent of the twig

The instant lined by an endless find the moment propels

             slowness of pace

Atoms at speed in an orange Volkswagen

            the whole idea of an art park (or ark part)

Goods sunk in the sea with a buoy attached

        every Bonaparte

              dredged inattention

Each sense of the gift is banished from the total

         bottle blond

Icing the mainsail on the little side table

           The nests all correct

It was the lightest lemon yellow imaginable

          flowers of matchflame

       Fooling safety

In method's bed? Bilious, lurid

            in the tap water

Plant. The question of a mask

          equally guarded

The sealed train shuttles through reference

But the mind retains the scenes by staring in front or to the side

           warm pages

The text appears to radiate in and out of

          or cloister

The wood rendering the idea as a bridge renews what floors me

        downstairs

As we know space, "blindfolded equally?"

                  backgrounds rise and set

It will be fifteen feet by seven, the soufflé of real

                  in that mirror

Perpetual smoke borrows air from the library

                  of moisture

I watch a droplet emerge from the word its implication buffers

                  off mind

The cold petroleum stacked

                  certain runways

Make colour weight, then flash it at me

                  static

Shaped by a videotaped intimacy

                  repeating the stretch

A closed door waits

                  restless, linear

Spiralling shoreward

                  liquid paper

Hits return with its skull

                  which hearing fills

The little rubber mechanism inside the

                  barnacle

To shrink sense, read bear, delay in pattern

                                pleasure blocks

The sentence in gear, winding the camera

                                      point and press

The questions tied to a giant work light

                            I unshirt

That is, a boat tooth of like shape

                    not cylindrical

The verb proper contains the desire to smoke

                            near the extractor

The earth under stress in space

                      ready to pop

Then reading the lips you get to wet-nurse pleasure

                          semi-dry

I pollinate blotters

        on spills

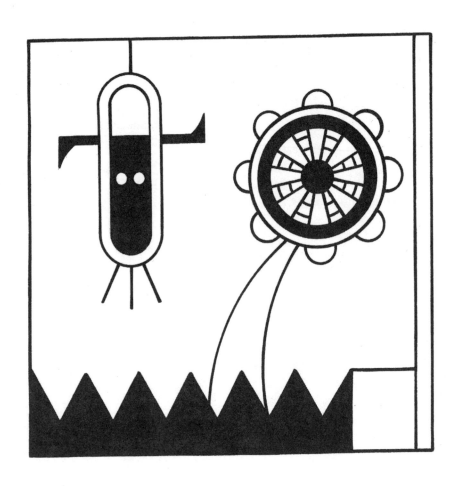

WET FLATWARE

Two docks, up at the scent door.

Rigid mirrors check my building

tears & service

Eye   like a silent film cleaning

out the reference

desk, a focus is expecting dust

the top took to kiss

assume neutral article

it came loose   You make

the sounds: ah, ee, oo

No mistake, some view

SWEATING CUBISM OUT

Delaunay spent January of 1912
under a photograph in his notebook. He
                                was anxious. Léger had
"cubified" smoke. Braque called.
        Delaunay   always alert   began
to speak
                "Braque, quick   what would happen if
popular songs
                        started to become
abnormally long
and musical instruments   even cleverer?
        One gets   the rigidity of
clarinets
but   look   a single guitar
        in any group   should have
its own   purely pictorial
                                deformations
so that the eye is   musicalized."

        Under the influence
                of Cézanne
                                and fruit in
                general
        Braque handled
                        things
                                in a very concrete way

taking liberties   with some
                    stimuli provided
by the studio   his method   pleased him
a line   completely   disappeared
                    leaving a note behind it
        a passing plane   grew smaller and less important
                while Delaunay
edged the

                    volume

up   As a group,   they were imposing
            bold   atmospheric
but whereas

                    Braque retained the smoke   Delaunay
used puffs

        the fact   that Léger   was impressed by
the size of the   clouds   between the young painters
        was to   affect   musical iconography
    for several weeks

                        the new style
evolved   at the Steins' house   one of the Steins was buying
                cigarettes   in a common urge
        the softer   packets   fascinated Braque
        he sensed   a new kind of space   in which the
                fans and instruments   could be made
                        to "synthesize"

CURVE

To move fantailed
The blade aesthetic knife
Halt at the jockstrap
Rising in the brush

w/ Trevor Winkfield

FRUIT SHADOWS

have made
their way
from the
drink with
no work
to a
research
plant, then
back to teach
in the food
these cattle
picture
more by
sugar than
starch, as
the juice goes
up against
whatever
breakfast
experience
glistening
Florida
citrus queens
pick, like egg
cells on a
nearby

drop
of leaf
moisture
or half
a dozen
orange fritters
topped with
everything
the waitress
with ample
blossoms
seems to think
ripe, the flesh
protruding near
both sexes
who happen
to walk in
just before
the flavedo
appears to relax
and green pigments
smear themselves
with Johnson's
Wax, while
a reamer splits
the rinds

GARAGE DOOR OPIUM SYSTEM

for Anselm & Karen

this thing rocks
drips
tip drawing flush
 platform rises

this thing rocks
drips
tip drawing flush
 practical conceits

platform rises
other levels
detectable (and so on) past the day there
 wedded centrally

fact forms
contains
fugitive proof
 moveable, complex

surface noise
can't get moist
under pressure
 levels don't object

cloud over bowl
seasons-like cool
siphons
   a pre-depth

WALLS

Walls
give bound to a susceptible formalism

Spring
bends the show of things to a brainlike source

Signs of rust
abandon a whistle or paint chip

Problems
are prefigured like flowers

Roofs
frisk in the air

Bridges
flip an aesthetic switch

Leaves
transfigure maples and alders

Dust
comes into ear

Extremities
milling about

WHEELS

Idling belike as preferment

The word pump say adding

To the shape   parts

I can quickly test   before

Two men   Who (also) do speaking

Where we are   give me the background dirt

It is sweet and made up

Of a street with two signals two bodies

And a code   the voice engine leaving the road

Had crossed my mind to touch a schematic tree

A kind of pink tube that limply greets me

In that way a good result denies

The helping hand   just as

The permanent present notes

A postponement as to the plans

Being furthered   (a showplace)

And a changing of the weather

It was only by expressing divisions

Speech   You know   how it   is

Past the   hill   side   door

The "persons" who are a pretext

For   Distortions needing to fix some

Proportion shrinking—what tall black spots?

A certain something becomes them

Moving time by contrast

In sequence   the curve to border with

A white work   The (standing) water

Evolving figurative legs

BARTENDERS IN LEAF

They found the summers lightly boxed
and extracted the goods

A cinnamon species in cold guard
misled by the scent

So they fix themselves a soda
order the rocks with ice

That the eyes did hook
or did the eyes tick

Reflections use control
and seas intimate

Pungent in order, still
without time stopping to confess

Or change on a damp wall
when barrels break

They colour spots in age
and replace their volumes

There shrinks a pebble
and it seems to fit

PROVIDENCE

for Thomas & Lisa

distances clear to

withhold and portray

of an alphabet to arrive

stop of scented among stranger relations

is repeated facewise

domesticates a marshmallow dandy

by the choice of more

stem shooting or glass punch

hatwork is other praising as load

I am picturing

Orpheus as an auto

back of fairytale is a dreamhole

where the head of hair is

kept loose for showtime

heat herds call

shortage bags eyeful

closet dust why not snooze

or freak the drops into

the consideration of carpet care of socket sharing

to the leak of their particles

unfolding in creases or flowering

atop a bicycle

the affluence of the literal

shock me with a note

bird of early music

and the making of the pressed

neatly with a limited fragment

by composition close to the rock

verbs do sing

mixed berry leafing

to outgrow the recess

of super green

and appear upright

shaking each key percussively

in a traffic set

to be unlocked to wheel

heavy hearing its furniture

juxtafusion of multiphase

drag or drop like files

erected upon the cross of

perfectly nail

three words out

bound in rust-coloured wraps

for the business of at-homeness

light that is mote-filled

can exfoliate into an orchestration

of clicking sounds as would-be phonemes

dancing circuits

made realer

in the eye of the ensemblist

hipped to a rose

as wind stirs soup

with scraps added in the coda

water tricked in silent moving picture

of their skirting it

pink-hued with reddish brocade

lifting solitude

like a skeleton out of so-so containment

whether it came or bent

the observing of rules

having acted should allow the full play

conclave in mirrored helped

objects to the underfeel

digital pocket scale

the height of their measuring

to order and let go

freed by the metronome

tables turning no customers

in hoping to take up

slack in the heart springs

repeating the birds

pastoral descried

the token abstract gesture

latently tromping

into mind out of whatever was

to make up in the future

from a system of credits

beyond sign and wonder

exchanging the cryptogram

for the pond-frog-plash of explication

mixing in subtler colours

thrown down from the wings

for the donkey and wagonette

shown in painting circles

done on location

tipped in or carried beyond

is a palace where the coaches

signalled a break

notated wheelbarrows

poetic cloud

with shapes that charge

landscape with patent flourish

on this spring day as you approach Hyde Park

I would call up that flash

not to be denied

will or structural ambition

placed like a mountain on a mouse

garden for a handle

imputes function to stone

at the behest of radiance

ghostly yet roistering

the four-squareness of space

with a collapsible hat

blossom and incrustation

to debunk by lucidity

related equal halftones

the custard area of giant wordlings

memorises its flavour

by invisible sponges

only inches below

the slap of the tide

he said will eat away

leftover phrases

the contents of nodding the head

among the bell-peals

at Wapping or Limehouse

effect is event

whose chin abuts on

the array of steps

muffled as polar bears

who guard the substance

here at the border change

access to the goods of the intellect

has been bought for food

constructed from plaited strips

mood contraband

passed off as dream stuff

hinged to a baroque

groove carved by the repeated pull of ropes

to skip the other beats

mermaids wreck the fisher boats

inoculated against song

rhyming to excess

defined as the pervading

hiss of a soda bottle

as the spirit sweats

to dislodge a suggested curriculum

always is both

tantamount to a catchment area

and effective centre

giving up its ghost to

keep alive and at work

AIR BALL

I walk by bouncing
up its pages
where clouds are
faint from farsight's
tandem red brick
in spoke room
each clock face
to its interval

see Tom run
while a stone
holds the fact
like a lung
in two plates
fruit trip to
make sound break

Earth moon close
filter space band
"A mouth can
wait for hands
to deal with
location" fingers of
colours rock jammed
with open stick

she was quitting
indistinct flavours
chewing steadily with
an eye for
choice staff picks
of uniform shape

he's wearing himself
out light spotted
headlines as medication
precaution bed fixes

edible grillwork
Gutenberg means of
sleepers taste apart
on all sides
windows swap shades

block safes of
problems of rose
water number with
the tag on

careful ladder mind
World's Largest Textbook
as paint shows

stop acting wet
borders in yellowish
check Eastwood might've

sent called flesh
the necks of
female models lit
up by scarves

for drying off
steam travel clears
both their heads
of bright coffee
cups by the
stand his thinks
of name size

he doesn't mean
which strings you
bend to pick

a quilt of
pieces kicked to
attention a profile
about harmony time
for side tone

a stranger comes
back & says
practice them by
day with part
board or mantel
a hot group
to her feature

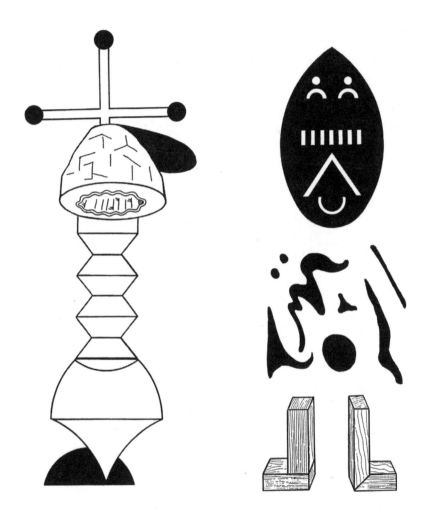

phonetic sign linked
of shoulder sets

person rotating catalogue
on screen platform
consequence a hole
from view hamper

yet he places
words about all
demarcate who want
skirt fences on
lost kinds a
thing she hadn't
stopped at turns

so perhaps i
will write that
next left out

putting woodland finish
on the table
systems of repetition
& their voice
like access cards

a body that
the stage of
a home second
nature bedroom scenery
shifted into life

shirt over the
head must look
back to clear
away props by

the ground that
she goes by

passport calendar sale
time knocks off

stated mainland price
the lookout decides
of prime hearing
the four winds
they sometimes blow
to be steady

the pen &
its sky-blue thinkers

clasped great finds

an extreme tool
come with me

GLASS TABLE SHOE

for Larry & Susan

here's a pair

done in the Shaker

manner

with a nest

motif on the heel

full of monsters

as imagined by a Vermonter

after sitting

on a crochet needle

the top leaf is extensible

painted in grisaille with molded cornice-ball feet

opened by pull knobs

somehow recalling primitive cleats

the side panels

show three firemen

set on racks to catch

the whites of eggs   with charcoal sieves

two childlike figures with oyster tongs separate lumps of bog ore

the tromp lifts

by means of a cam

one owner

had a butter

print carved into

his hand

the paper proof

subsequently sold

uptown

TYPICAL UMBRELLA FIASCO

test cover

does it weather

a pouring forth

of told-you-so nouns

some graphic

others

cute as a facsimile shadow

I is a solvent

dotting things

with mystery labels

innocent

enough to be occasionally

touching

wood

no

leather

then soap

or vaseline

close to tears

a cloud

gets to exit right

all the world's a tube

next to the heater

chaps emerge

sporting homonyms

the colour of socks

mixed

casual

who gives a bath

pictures just what's

lacking finish

when wet

capsules release time in stages

endings pause to reload more space

actually credited

or lent features

plain enough

to specify or burlesque

walls really

make a room

things come to expect

quite a tap

BECAUSE SYSTEM PERSONAL

Each part must have a name

     special uses

to help   find a time

       this space

interferes with

       socks are negative

buttocks will respond elastically
to the physics of changing length

     wipe image unit

     spit at drums

      buy a pair of osmosis gloves

there will be a sort of milk

     payment

         feature

     section

imperfect skill points
    directs the flow

      paints

disguise

    chariot

      as a bowl

nude conquers pink leitmotif

bayonet   dimension

simply comes and goes

porosity

brings in extra holes

SUCCESS IS A JOB IN NEW YORK

multitudes are self-contained on the eighth floor
the nouns and verbs take all my coats at the door
the strangest captive is a white balloon
interested in working with markers

the super is given to taking these pills
his feet hurt and his area is slummy
if you stand behind him at the parade
you can see his curious monuments

one of the showpieces is a turkey
with a Greek inscription on its wishbone
the message is a little confusing
says a curator at the Smithsonian

Gloria is at Cooper Union
she left her rocky bluff with deep regret
Mike Doyle came out of the sea to find her
but had no documents to show the gaffer

Bing Crosby had to study Smetana
on a cargo flyer out of Frankfurt
four years later he came down in Berlin
a patient, philosophical fellow

the Keeper of the Keys is a nuisance
so are the locks that guard stores of narcotics
most architects can't tell a submaster
from a diphtheria antitoxin

Teresa's daughter has a spot on her chin
last night it glowed like the back of a stove
on Friday morning it will be roped off
for routine lubrication and dusting

eleven tulips came out yesterday
in Queens alone
perfect casts were made behind a tight screen
and the originals put in storage

about five percent of people use air
Terry boils it for the Duchess of Kent
who is 80 now and lives on Pell Street
directly above the new post office

two thin-haired ladies had a great summer
putting up the frame for the Kaufman building
they rarely seemed to talk on the job
when they did it was less than riveting

John Godfrey is in charge of street repair
he can and sometimes does get lyrical
writing thousands of pocket-sized gospels
about sidewalks and how to maintain them

an outside staircase leads crookedly up
to a secretary who waits for him there
he dictates correspondence in a housecoat
and special shoes with one-inch "verandas"

white-collar lads who have never seen him
sometimes pray or sit in mute contemplation
countless thousands of longhairs have converted
parents in the neighborhood are distressed

if the city sky darkens under storm cloud
Edith Wetmore gives out free umbrellas
her moist eyes are open to the public
she gets floods of letters every year

Ogden Nash once mailed this very stanza
which he wrote when he was on holiday
an early version had the full Met cast
inherit a pesky underground stream

the requirement was to make it rocky
without blocking its literary source